the joy of
BELIEVE
christmas

SELECTIONS FROM THE
NEW INTERNATIONAL VERSION

the joy of

BELIEVE

christmas

GENERAL EDITOR
RANDY FRAZEE

ZONDERVAN®

ZONDERVAN
Believe: The Joy of Christmas
Copyright © 2014 by Zondervan

Requests for information should be addressed to:
Zondervan, 3900 *Sparks Drive SE, Grand Rapids, Michigan,* 49546

Cover design: Extra Credit Projects

Printed in the United States of America

14 15 16 17 18 19 20 /OPM/ 10 9 8 7 6 5 4 3 2 1

Table of Contents

Foreword

An angel of the Lord appeared to them,
and the glory of the Lord shone
around them, and they were terrified.
But the angel said to them, "Do not be afraid.
I bring you good news that will cause
great joy for all the people. Today in the
town of David a Savior has been born to you;
he is the Messiah, the Lord."
Luke 2:9 – 11

Let me ask you a question. Are you a part of the "all" in the words "all the people"? Then this promise was meant for you. When Jesus entered our world wrapped in swaddling clothes and lying in a manger, it was God the Father's intent for this to bring you joy.

Maybe this Christmas season joy has passed you over. It doesn't have to be this way. God's promise is still alive, and his offer of joy is still available to you.

This little book aims to help. It is a collection of Scripture stories from Genesis to Revelation built around three key themes of the Christian life — Beliefs, Practices and Virtues. All three hold the secret to God's offer of joy.

BELIEFS — PERSONAL GOD

Experiencing joy begins by believing God is involved in and cares about your daily life. Do you believe this?

PRACTICES — PRAYER

For a belief to have a full impact on us, we can't just believe it in our heads; we must also believe it in our hearts. This spiritual practice will help the belief above take the 12-inch journey from the head to the heart.

VIRTUES — JOY

Over time the fruit of joy will appear in your life. God's joy enables you to experience inner contentment and purpose amid your circumstances — both good and bad. How about that?

Bask in the gift of God's Word this Christmas, and before long you will be singing, "Joy to the world, the Lord has come."

— Randy Frazee
General Editor

CHAPTER

1

Personal God

KEY IDEA

I believe God is involved in and cares
about my daily life.

KEY VERSE

I lift up my eyes to the mountains —
where does my help come from?
My help comes from the LORD,
the Maker of heaven and earth.
Psalm 121:1–2

The God of the Bible is the only true God—
Father, Son and Holy Spirit. He is the one all-
powerful, all-knowing eternal God. But is he
good? Is he involved in his creation? Does he
love us? Does he have a plan for us? Is he inter-
ceding and intervening to move the events of
our life and world toward his intended purpose?
Consider the following stories and decide for
yourself.

God Is Good

Abraham and Sarah—the great patriarch and
matriarch of the Israelite people—were first
named Abram and Sarai. God had promised
Abraham that he would be the father of a great
nation, but how can you father a nation when
you have no children?

Now Sarai, Abram's wife, had borne him no children. But she had an Egyptian slave named Hagar; so she said to Abram, "The LORD has kept me from having children. Go, sleep with my slave; perhaps I can build a family through her."

Abram agreed to what Sarai said. So after Abram had been living in Canaan ten years, Sarai his wife took her Egyptian slave Hagar and gave her to her husband to be his wife. He slept with Hagar, and she conceived.

When she knew she was pregnant, she began to despise her mistress. Then Sarai said to Abram,

"You are responsible for the wrong I am suffering. I put my slave in your arms, and now that she knows she is pregnant, she despises me. May the LORD judge between you and me."

"Your slave is in your hands," Abram said. "Do with her whatever you think best." Then Sarai mistreated Hagar; so she fled from her.

The angel of the LORD found Hagar near a spring in the desert; it was the spring that is beside the road to Shur. And he said, "Hagar, slave of Sarai, where have you come from, and where are you going?"

"I'm running away from my mistress Sarai," she answered.

Then the angel of the LORD told her, "Go back to your mistress and submit to her." The angel added, "I will increase your descendants so much that they will be too numerous to count."

The angel of the LORD also said to her:

> "You are now pregnant
>   and you will give birth to a son.
> You shall name him Ishmael,
>   for the LORD has heard of your misery.
> He will be a wild donkey of a man;
>   his hand will be against everyone
>   and everyone's hand against him,
> and he will live in hostility
>   toward all his brothers."

She gave this name to the LORD who spoke to her: "You are the God who sees me," for she said, "I have now seen the One who sees me." That is why the well was called Beer Lahai Roi; it is still there, between Kadesh and Bered.

So Hagar bore Abram a son, and Abram gave the name Ishmael to the son she had borne. Abram was eighty-six years old when Hagar bore him Ishmael.

Abraham and Sarah had tried to "help God out" by having Abraham father a child with Hagar. What resulted was a debacle for everyone involved. But in this story, we see the beginning of a pattern—God takes our messes and turns them into something good. Hagar involuntarily became party to Abraham's and Sarah's lack of faith. Yet God heard her cries and helped her. The story continues ...

Now the LORD was gracious to Sarah as he had said, and the LORD did for Sarah what he had promised. Sarah became pregnant and bore a son to Abraham in his old age, at the very time God had promised him. Abraham gave the name Isaac to the son Sarah bore him. When his son Isaac was eight days old, Abraham circumcised him, as God commanded him. Abraham was a hundred years old when his son Isaac was born to him.

Sarah said, "God has brought me laughter, and everyone who hears about this will laugh with me." And she added, "Who would have said to Abraham that Sarah would nurse children? Yet I have borne him a son in his old age."

The child grew and was weaned, and on the day Isaac was weaned Abraham held a great feast. But Sarah saw that the son whom Hagar the Egyptian had borne to Abraham was mocking, and she said to Abraham, "Get rid of that slave woman and her son, for that woman's son will never share in the inheritance with my son Isaac."

The matter distressed Abraham greatly because it concerned his son. But God said to him, "Do not be so distressed about the boy and your slave woman. Listen to whatever Sarah tells you, because it is through Isaac that your offspring will be reckoned. I will make the son of the slave into a nation also, because he is your offspring."

Early the next morning Abraham took some food and a skin of water and gave them to Hagar. He set them on her shoulders and then sent her off with the boy. She went on her way and wandered in the Desert of Beersheba.

When the water in the skin was gone, she put the boy under one of the bushes. Then she went off and sat down about a bowshot away, for she thought, "I cannot watch the boy die." And as she sat there, she began to sob.

God heard the boy crying, and the angel of God called to Hagar from heaven and said to her, "What is the matter, Hagar? Do not be afraid; God has heard the boy crying as he lies there. Lift the boy up and take him by the hand, for I will make him into a great nation."

Then God opened her eyes and she saw a well of water. So she went and filled the skin with water and gave the boy a drink.

God was with the boy as he grew up. He lived in the desert and became an archer. While he was living in the Desert of Paran, his mother got a wife for him from Egypt.

In the story of Hagar and Ishmael, even though they were on the wrong side of God's perfect plan, in his goodness, God provided for and blessed them (and even their descendants).

Another Biblical character in whose life we see how much God is involved and cares about his people is David, the poet, singer, shepherd, warrior and king, who wrote and sang from a deep well as he journeyed through life and encountered the one true God. David composed many of the psalms found in our Bible. David wrote as a shepherd boy while gazing at the billions of stars God created; he wrote while being chased down by King Saul; he wrote while he was king of Israel; and he wrote as he was coming to the end of his life on earth. The songs that David and the other psalmists wrote express their personal and intimate relationship with God.

LORD, our Lord,
how majestic is your name in all
the earth!

You have set your glory
in the heavens.
Through the praise of children and
infants
you have established a stronghold
against your enemies,
to silence the foe and the avenger.
When I consider your heavens,
the work of your fingers,
the moon and the stars,
which you have set in place,
what is mankind that you are mindful
of them,
human beings that you care for them?

You have made them a little lower than
the angels
and crowned them with glory and
honor.
You made them rulers over the works of
your hands;
you put everything under their feet:

all flocks and herds,
    and the animals of the wild,
the birds in the sky,
    and the fish in the sea,
    all that swim the paths of the
        seas.

LORD, our Lord,
    how majestic is your name in all
        the earth!

The LORD is my shepherd, I lack
        nothing.
    He makes me lie down in green
        pastures,
he leads me beside quiet waters,
    he refreshes my soul.
He guides me along the right paths
    for his name's sake.
Even though I walk
    through the darkest valley,
I will fear no evil,
    for you are with me;
your rod and your staff,
    they comfort me.

You prepare a table before me
    in the presence of my enemies.
You anoint my head with oil;
    my cup overflows.

Surely your goodness and love will
     follow me
  all the days of my life,
and I will dwell in the house of the LORD
  forever.

You have searched me, LORD,
  and you know me.
You know when I sit and when I rise;
  you perceive my thoughts from afar.
You discern my going out and my lying
     down;
  you are familiar with all my ways.
Before a word is on my tongue
  you, LORD, know it completely.
You hem me in behind and before,
  and you lay your hand upon me.
Such knowledge is too wonderful for me,
  too lofty for me to attain.

Where can I go from your Spirit?
  Where can I flee from your presence?
If I go up to the heavens, you are there;
  if I make my bed in the depths, you are
     there.
If I rise on the wings of the dawn,
  if I settle on the far side of the sea,
even there your hand will guide me,
  your right hand will hold me fast.

If I say, "Surely the darkness will hide me
   and the light become night around me,"
even the darkness will not be dark
      to you;
   the night will shine like the day,
   for darkness is as light to you.

For you created my inmost being;
   you knit me together in my mother's
      womb.
I praise you because I am fearfully and
      wonderfully made;
   your works are wonderful,
   I know that full well.
My frame was not hidden from you
   when I was made in the secret place,
   when I was woven together in the
      depths of the earth.
Your eyes saw my unformed body;
   all the days ordained for me were
      written in your book
   before one of them came to be.
How precious to me are your thoughts,
      God!
   How vast is the sum of them!
Were I to count them,
   they would outnumber the grains
      of sand —
   when I awake, I am still with you.

If only you, God, would slay the wicked!
    Away from me, you who are
        bloodthirsty!
They speak of you with evil intent;
    your adversaries misuse your name.
Do I not hate those who hate you,
        Lord,
    and abhor those who are in rebellion
        against you?
I have nothing but hatred for them;
    I count them my enemies.
Search me, God, and know my heart;
    test me and know my anxious
        thoughts.
See if there is any offensive way in me,
    and lead me in the way everlasting.

I will exalt you, my God the King;
    I will praise your name for ever and
        ever.
Every day I will praise you
    and extol your name for ever and ever.

Great is the Lord and most worthy of
        praise;
    his greatness no one can fathom.
One generation commends your works to
        another;
    they tell of your mighty acts.

They speak of the glorious splendor of
> your majesty —
> and I will meditate on your wonderful
> works.
They tell of the power of your awesome
> works —
> and I will proclaim your great deeds.
They celebrate your abundant goodness
> and joyfully sing of your righteousness.

The LORD is gracious and compassionate,
> slow to anger and rich in love.

The LORD is good to all;
> he has compassion on all he has made.
All your works praise you, LORD;
> your faithful people extol you.
They tell of the glory of your kingdom
> and speak of your might,
so that all people may know of your
> mighty acts
> and the glorious splendor of your
> kingdom.
Your kingdom is an everlasting kingdom,
> and your dominion endures through all
> generations.

The LORD is trustworthy in all he
> promises
> and faithful in all he does.

The LORD upholds all who fall
and lifts up all who are bowed down.
The eyes of all look to you,
and you give them their food at the
proper time.
You open your hand
and satisfy the desires of every living
thing.

The LORD is righteous in all his ways
and faithful in all he does.
The LORD is near to all who call on him,
to all who call on him in truth.
He fulfills the desires of those who fear
him;
he hears their cry and saves them.
The LORD watches over all who love him,
but all the wicked he will destroy.

My mouth will speak in praise of the LORD.
Let every creature praise his holy name
for ever and ever.

GOD HAS A PLAN

Forty years after the death of David, the nation of Israel was torn in two, and what resulted were two nations: the northern kingdom of Israel and the southern kingdom of Judah. All the kings of Israel did evil in the eyes of the Lord. In Judah, only a handful of kings were good. One of them was Hezekiah. He courageously served the Lord in perilous times.

Then when he was about 38 years old, Hezekiah became ill and was about to die. He was devastated and pleaded with the Lord for mercy. In response, the Lord sent him a shocking message and a tender change of plan. We know from the Bible that God has a plan for our individual lives and has our days numbered. This story shows how God will hear our prayers and see our tears. He may not answer us in the way we desire, but he will sometimes alter the plan he has for us at the request of his children.

In those days Hezekiah became ill and was at the point of death. The prophet Isaiah son of Amoz went to him and said, "This is what the LORD says: Put your house in order, because you are going to die; you will not recover."

Hezekiah turned his face to the wall and prayed to the LORD, "Remember, LORD, how I have walked before you faithfully and with whole-hearted devotion and have done what is good in your eyes." And Hezekiah wept bitterly.

Before Isaiah had left the middle court, the word of the LORD came to him: "Go back and tell Hezekiah, the ruler of my people, 'This is what the LORD, the God of your father David, says: I have heard your prayer and seen your tears; I will heal you. On the third day from now you will go up to the temple of the LORD. I will add fifteen years to your life. And I will deliver you and this city from the hand of the king of Assyria. I will defend this city for my sake and for the sake of my servant David.'"

Then Isaiah said, "Prepare a poultice of figs." They did so and applied it to the boil, and he recovered.

While Hezekiah's story focuses on the length of his life, Jeremiah's story goes all the way back before he was born. Jeremiah was a prophet who lived in the time of the divided kingdom. He lived in the southern kingdom of Judah and prophesied to the people there of their coming conquest and exile by the Babylonians. In both Hezekiah's life and Jeremiah's, God is not distant or ambivalent, but near and loving.

The words of Jeremiah son of Hilkiah, one of the priests at Anathoth in the territory of Benjamin. The word of the LORD came to him in the thirteenth year of the reign of Josiah son of Amon king of Judah, and through the reign of Jehoiakim son of Josiah king of Judah, down to the fifth month of the eleventh year of Zedekiah son of Josiah king of Judah, when the people of Jerusalem went into exile.

The word of the LORD came to me, saying,

> "Before I formed you in the womb I knew
> you,
> before you were born I set you apart;
> I appointed you as a prophet to the
> nations."

"Alas, Sovereign LORD," I said, "I do not know how to speak; I am too young."

But the LORD said to me, "Do not say, 'I am too young.' You must go to everyone I send you to and say whatever I command you. Do not be afraid of them, for I am with you and will rescue you," declares the LORD.

Then the LORD reached out his hand and touched my mouth and said to me, "I have put my words in your mouth. See, today I appoint you over nations and kingdoms to uproot and tear down, to destroy and overthrow, to build and to plant."

The word of the LORD came to me: "What do you see, Jeremiah?"

"I see the branch of an almond tree," I replied.

The LORD said to me, "You have seen correctly, for I am watching to see that my word is fulfilled."

The word of the LORD came to me again: "What do you see?"

"I see a pot that is boiling," I answered. "It is tilting toward us from the north."

The LORD said to me, "From the north disaster will be poured out on all who live in the land. I am about to summon all the peoples of the northern kingdoms," declares the LORD.

> "Their kings will come and set up their
> thrones
>   in the entrance of the gates of
>   Jerusalem;
> they will come against all her surrounding
> walls
>   and against all the towns of Judah.
> I will pronounce my judgments on my
> people
>   because of their wickedness in
>   forsaking me,
> in burning incense to other gods
>   and in worshiping what their hands
>   have made.

"Get yourself ready! Stand up and say to them whatever I command you. Do not be terrified by them, or I will terrify you before them. Today I have made you a fortified city, an iron pillar and a bronze wall to stand against the whole land — against the kings of Judah, its officials, its priests and the people of the land. They will fight against you but will not overcome you, for I am with you and will rescue you," declares the LORD.

Jeremiah's calling was very specific to the overall plan God was revealing through Israel. He faithfully warned the southern kingdom of Judah about their unfaithfulness and God's pending discipline. He knew up front that they would not listen, but his task was simply to be faithful and courageous and to deliver the message from God. Three times the dreaded Babylonians attacked Jerusalem and carried away some of the people to Babylon. In 597, after the second deportation, God gave Jeremiah the assignment of writing a letter to those exiles to remind them that, as Jeremiah had experienced personally, God has a grand and good plan for their lives.

This is the text of the letter that the prophet Jeremiah sent from Jerusalem to the surviving elders among the exiles and to the priests, the prophets and all the other people Nebuchadnezzar had carried into exile from Jerusalem to Babylon. (This was after King Jehoiachin and the queen mother, the court officials and the leaders of Judah and Jerusalem, the skilled workers and the artisans had gone into exile from Jerusalem.) He entrusted the letter to Elasah son of Shaphan and to Gemariah son of Hilkiah, whom Zedekiah king of Judah sent to King Nebuchadnezzar in Babylon. It said:

This is what the LORD Almighty, the God of Israel, says to all those I carried into exile from Jerusalem to Babylon: "Build houses and settle down; plant gardens and eat what they produce. Marry and have sons and daughters; find wives for your sons and give your daughters in marriage, so that they too may have sons and daughters. Increase in number there; do not decrease. Also, seek the peace and prosperity of the city to which I have carried you into exile. Pray to the LORD for it, because if it prospers, you too will prosper." Yes, this is what the LORD Almighty, the God of Israel, says: "Do not let the prophets and diviners among you deceive you. Do not listen to the dreams you encourage them to have. They are prophesying lies to you in my name. I have not sent them," declares the LORD.

This is what the LORD says: "When seventy years are completed for Babylon, I will come to you and fulfill my good promise to bring you back to this place. For I know the plans I have for you," declares the LORD, "plans to prosper you and not to harm you, plans to give you hope and a future. Then you will call on me and come and pray to me, and I will listen to you. You will seek me and find me when you seek me with all your heart. I will be found by you," declares the LORD, "and will bring you back from captivity. I will gather you from all the nations and places where I have banished you," declares the LORD, "and will bring you back to the place from which I carried you into exile."

GOD CARES FOR US

Jesus, the Son of God, came to earth. He was born as a human baby and lived among us. His arrival removes any doubt about the nearness of God in our lives. Jesus is Immanuel, "God with us."

When a large crowd assembled on a hillside by the Sea of Galilee, Jesus taught this weary and worn bunch about the intricate involvement of God in their lives.

"Therefore I tell you, do not worry about your life, what you will eat or drink; or about your body, what you will wear. Is not life more than food, and the body more than clothes? Look at the birds of the air; they do not sow or reap or store away in barns, and yet your heavenly Father feeds them. Are you not much more valuable than they? Can any one of you by worrying add a single hour to your life?

"And why do you worry about clothes? See how the flowers of the field grow. They do not labor or spin. Yet I tell you that not even Solomon in all his splendor was dressed like one of these. If that is how God clothes the grass of the field, which is here today and tomorrow is thrown into the fire, will he not much more clothe you — you of little faith? So do not worry, saying, 'What shall we eat?' or 'What shall we drink?' or 'What shall we wear?' For the pagans run after all these things, and your heavenly Father knows that you need them. But seek first his kingdom and his righteousness, and all these things will be given to you as well. Therefore do not worry about tomorrow, for tomorrow will worry about itself. Each day has enough trouble of its own."

After Jesus' death on the cross, he ascended back to the Father in heaven. Then God the Holy Spirit descended on all who believed in Jesus. The dwelling place for God was no longer in temples built by human hands but in the very inner spirits of his people. From the inside out the Holy Spirit speaks to us, ministers to us, affirms us, directs us, challenges us and empowers us. With pen in hand, the apostle Paul instructed the church that gathered in Rome of this great truth.

Therefore, brothers and sisters, we have an obligation — but it is not to the flesh, to live according to it. For if you live according to the flesh, you will die; but if by the Spirit you put to death the misdeeds of the body, you will live.

For those who are led by the Spirit of God are the children of God. The Spirit you received does not make you slaves, so that you live in fear again; rather, the Spirit you received brought about your adoption to sonship. And by him we cry, *"Abba,* Father." The Spirit himself testifies with our spirit that we are God's children. Now if we are children, then we are heirs — heirs of God and co-heirs with Christ, if indeed we share in his sufferings in order that we may also share in his glory.

I consider that our present sufferings are not worth comparing with the glory that will be revealed in us. For the creation waits in eager expectation for the children of God to be revealed. For the creation was subjected to frustration, not by its own choice, but by the will of the one who subjected it, in hope that the creation itself will be liberated from its bondage to decay and brought into the freedom and glory of the children of God.

We know that the whole creation has been groaning as in the pains of childbirth right up to the present time. Not only so, but we ourselves, who have the firstfruits of the Spirit, groan inwardly as we wait eagerly for our adoption to sonship, the redemption of our bodies. For in this hope we were saved. But hope that is seen is no hope at all. Who hopes for what they already have? But if we hope for what we do not yet have, we wait for it patiently.

In the same way, the Spirit helps us in our weakness. We do not know what we ought to pray for, but the Spirit himself intercedes for us through wordless groans. And he who searches our hearts knows the mind of the Spirit, because the Spirit intercedes for God's people in accordance with the will of God.

And we know that in all things God works for the good of those who love him, who have been called according to his purpose. For those God foreknew he also predestined to be conformed to the image of his Son, that he might be the firstborn among many brothers and sisters. And those he predestined, he also called; those he called, he also justified; those he justified, he also glorified.

What, then, shall we say in response to these things? If God is for us, who can be against us? He who did not spare his own Son, but gave him up for us all — how will he not also, along with him, graciously give us all things? Who will bring any charge against those whom God has chosen? It is God who justifies. Who then is the one who condemns? No one. Christ Jesus who died — more than that, who was raised to life — is at the right hand of God and is also interceding for us. Who shall separate us from the love of Christ? Shall trouble or hardship or persecution or famine or nakedness or danger or sword? As it is written:

"For your sake we face death all day long;
we are considered as sheep to be
slaughtered."

No, in all these things we are more than conquerors through him who loved us. For I am convinced that neither death nor life, neither angels nor demons, neither the present nor the future, nor any powers, neither height nor depth, nor anything else in all creation, will be able to separate us from the love of God that is in Christ Jesus our Lord.

What amazing love God has for his people! In the spirit of this love, James, the half brother of Jesus, wrote a practical letter to Jesus' early disciples. He reminded them that God is involved in and cares about their daily lives—although they too had a role to play. As believers, we can acknowledge God's involvement in our lives, even during seasons of trial. We can seek God and ask him for wisdom. We must also be careful not to blame God for our trials and temptations and realize that every good gift comes from his hand.

James, a servant of God and of the Lord Jesus Christ,

To the twelve tribes scattered among the nations:

Greetings.

Consider it pure joy, my brothers and sisters, whenever you face trials of many kinds, because you know that the testing of your faith produces perseverance. Let perseverance finish its work so that you may be mature and complete, not lacking anything. If any of you lacks wisdom, you should ask God, who gives generously to all without finding fault, and it will be given to you. But when you ask, you must believe and not doubt, because the one who doubts is like a wave of the sea, blown and tossed by the wind. That person should not expect to receive anything from the Lord. Such a person is double-minded and unstable in all they do.

Believers in humble circumstances ought to take pride in their high position. But the rich should take pride in their humiliation — since they will pass away like a wild flower. For the sun rises with scorching heat and withers the plant; its blossom falls and its beauty is destroyed. In the same way, the rich will fade away even while they go about their business.

Blessed is the one who perseveres under trial because, having stood the test, that person will receive the crown of life that the Lord has promised to those who love him.

When tempted, no one should say, "God is

tempting me." For God cannot be tempted by evil, nor does he tempt anyone; but each person is tempted when they are dragged away by their own evil desire and enticed. Then, after desire has conceived, it gives birth to sin; and sin, when it is full-grown, gives birth to death.

Don't be deceived, my dear brothers and sisters. Every good and perfect gift is from above, coming down from the Father of the heavenly lights, who does not change like shifting shadows. He chose to give us birth through the word of truth, that we might be a kind of firstfruits of all he created.

CHAPTER

2

Worship

KEY IDEA

I worship God for who he is
and what he has done for me.

KEY VERSE

Come, let us sing for joy to the LORD;
let us shout aloud to the Rock of our salvation.
Let us come before him with thanksgiving
and extol him with music and song.
Psalm 95:1–2

Worshiping God for who he is and what he has done for us can be expressed in many different forms and diverse environments, but it's the heart behind the actions that matters to God. Throughout Scripture we see how God's people worshiped him on towering mountaintops, inside homes with dirt floors, at a lavishly adorned temple and in dark prisons. They demonstrated their devotion to God with singing, dancing, sacrifices and public and private prayer. What's most important to God is not the way that we choose to worship him, but the motivation that directs our actions.

THE HEART'S INTENT

Come, let us sing for joy to the LORD;
>   let us shout aloud to the Rock of our
>   salvation.
Let us come before him with thanksgiving
>   and extol him with music and song.

For the LORD is the great God,
>   the great King above all gods.
In his hand are the depths of the earth,
>   and the mountain peaks belong to him.
The sea is his, for he made it,
>   and his hands formed the dry land.

Come, let us bow down in worship,
>   let us kneel before the LORD our Maker;

for he is our God
and we are the people of his pasture,
the flock under his care.

During Old Testament times, worship involved animal sacrifices. Instead of leaving his people with no recourse except to face their punishment for sin, God, in his mercy, allowed his people to sacrifice the best animal from their herd as a payment for their disobedience. The animal had to be without defect, since a defective sacrifice could not be a substitute for a defective people. This practice was intended to be accompanied by repentance. The worshiper confessed their sin and laid hands on the animal; then the sin was symbolically transferred away from the sinner to the sacrifice.

Unfortunately, over time the Israelites' sacrifices became meaningless rituals. God was angry and heartbroken. The people brought him an abundance of sacrifices, yet their character and conduct were anything but pleasing to him.

"The multitude of your sacrifices —
what are they to me?" says the LORD.
"I have more than enough of burnt
offerings,
of rams and the fat of fattened animals;

I have no pleasure
   in the blood of bulls and lambs and
      goats.
When you come to appear before me,
   who has asked this of you,
   this trampling of my courts?
Stop bringing meaningless offerings!
   Your incense is detestable to me.
New Moons, Sabbaths and
      convocations —
   I cannot bear your worthless
     assemblies.
Your New Moon feasts and your
     appointed festivals
   I hate with all my being.
They have become a burden to me;
   I am weary of bearing them.
When you spread out your hands in
     prayer,
   I hide my eyes from you;
even when you offer many prayers,
   I am not listening.

Your hands are full of blood!

Wash and make yourselves clean.
   Take your evil deeds out of my sight;
   stop doing wrong.
Learn to do right; seek justice.
   Defend the oppressed.

Take up the cause of the fatherless;
    plead the case of the widow.

"Come now, let us settle the matter,"
    says the LORD.
"Though your sins are like scarlet,
    they shall be as white as snow;
though they are red as crimson,
    they shall be like wool.
If you are willing and obedient,
    you will eat the good things of the land;
but if you resist and rebel,
    you will be devoured by the sword."
                For the mouth of the LORD
                    has spoken.

In the New Testament, those who failed to worship and honor God properly received some harsh words from Jesus. This was especially true for the religious leaders whose layers of religious exercises and rituals hid a weak and shallow faith. As a crowd gathered to listen to Jesus' teachings, he warned them about the influence of these hollow religious leaders.

Then Jesus said to the crowds and to his disciples: "The teachers of the law and the Pharisees sit in Moses' seat. So you must be careful to do everything they tell you. But do not do what they do, for they do not practice what they preach. They tie up heavy, cumbersome loads and put them on other people's shoulders, but they themselves are not willing to lift a finger to move them.

"Everything they do is done for people to see: They make their phylacteries wide and the tassels on their garments long; they love the place of honor at banquets and the most important seats in the synagogues; they love to be greeted with respect in the marketplaces and to be called 'Rabbi' by others.

"But you are not to be called 'Rabbi,' for you have one Teacher, and you are all brothers. And do not call anyone on earth 'father,' for you have one Father, and he is in heaven. Nor are you to be called instructors, for you have one Instructor, the Messiah. The greatest among you will be your servant. For those who exalt themselves will be humbled, and those who humble themselves will be exalted.

"Woe to you, teachers of the law and Pharisees, you hypocrites! You shut the door of the kingdom of heaven in people's faces. You yourselves do not enter, nor will you let those enter who are trying to.

"Woe to you, teachers of the law and Pharisees, you hypocrites! You travel over land and sea to win a single convert, and when you have succeeded, you make them twice as much a child of hell as you are.

"Woe to you, blind guides! You say, 'If anyone swears by the temple, it means nothing; but anyone who swears by the gold of the temple is bound by that oath.' You blind fools! Which is greater: the gold, or the temple that makes the gold sacred? You also say, 'If anyone swears by the altar, it means nothing; but anyone who swears by the gift on the altar is bound by that oath.' You blind men! Which is greater: the gift, or the altar that makes the gift sacred? Therefore, anyone who swears by the altar swears by it and by everything on it. And anyone who swears by the temple swears by it and by the one who dwells in it. And anyone who swears by heaven swears by God's throne and by the one who sits on it.

"Woe to you, teachers of the law and Pharisees, you hypocrites! You give a tenth of your spices — mint, dill and cumin. But you have neglected the more important matters of the law — justice, mercy and faithfulness. You should have practiced the latter, without neglecting the former. You blind guides! You strain out a gnat but swallow a camel.

"Woe to you, teachers of the law and Pharisees, you hypocrites! You clean the outside of the cup and dish, but inside they are full of greed and self-indulgence. Blind Pharisee! First clean the inside of the cup and dish, and then the outside also will be clean.

"Woe to you, teachers of the law and Pharisees,

you hypocrites! You are like whitewashed tombs, which look beautiful on the outside but on the inside are full of the bones of the dead and everything unclean. In the same way, on the outside you appear to people as righteous but on the inside you are full of hypocrisy and wickedness."

UNASHAMED WORSHIPERS

When God calls us to love him with all our heart, soul, mind and strength, he is demanding that we hold nothing back from him. A commitment to worship God is a vow to be bold and unashamed of our love and devotion to him. With great power, God rescued the Israelites when the army of Egypt had them backed against the Red Sea. After their escape, Moses and his sister Miriam led the Israelites in an unapologetic song of celebration and blessing, praising God for who he is and what he had done for them.

Then Moses and the Israelites sang this song to the LORD:

> "I will sing to the LORD,
>   for he is highly exalted.
> Both horse and driver
>   he has hurled into the sea.
>
> "The LORD is my strength and my defense;
>   he has become my salvation.

He is my God, and I will praise him,
   my father's God, and I will exalt him.
The LORD is a warrior;
   the LORD is his name.
Pharaoh's chariots and his army
   he has hurled into the sea.
The best of Pharaoh's officers
   are drowned in the Red Sea.
The deep waters have covered them;
   they sank to the depths like a stone.
Your right hand, LORD,
   was majestic in power.
Your right hand, LORD,
   shattered the enemy.

"In the greatness of your majesty
   you threw down those who opposed
      you.
You unleashed your burning anger;
   it consumed them like stubble.
By the blast of your nostrils
   the waters piled up.
The surging waters stood up like a wall;
   the deep waters congealed in the heart
      of the sea.
The enemy boasted,
   'I will pursue, I will overtake them.
I will divide the spoils;
   I will gorge myself on them.

I will draw my sword
   and my hand will destroy them.'
But you blew with your breath,
   and the sea covered them.
They sank like lead
   in the mighty waters.
Who among the gods
   is like you, LORD?
Who is like you —
   majestic in holiness,
awesome in glory,
   working wonders?

"You stretch out your right hand,
   and the earth swallows your enemies.
In your unfailing love you will lead
   the people you have redeemed.
In your strength you will guide them
   to your holy dwelling.
The nations will hear and tremble;
   anguish will grip the people of
      Philistia.
The chiefs of Edom will be terrified,
   the leaders of Moab will be seized with
      trembling,
the people of Canaan will melt away;
   terror and dread will fall on them.
By the power of your arm
   they will be as still as a stone —

until your people pass by, LORD,
    until the people you bought pass by.
You will bring them in and plant them
    on the mountain of your inheritance —
the place, LORD, you made for your
        dwelling,
    the sanctuary, Lord, your hands
        established.

"The LORD reigns
    for ever and ever."

When Pharaoh's horses, chariots and horsemen went into the sea, the LORD brought the waters of the sea back over them, but the Israelites walked through the sea on dry ground. Then Miriam the prophet, Aaron's sister, took a timbrel in her hand, and all the women followed her, with timbrels and dancing. Miriam sang to them:

"Sing to the LORD,
    for he is highly exalted.
Both horse and driver
    he has hurled into the sea."

While Moses and Miriam expressed their praise vocally, bold worship can also be displayed with very few words. Take Daniel, for example. His quiet refusal to worship anyone or anything but the one true God was a risky decision because King Darius dealt harshly with disobedience in his kingdom. Unlike the songs of Moses and Miriam, it was Daniel's actions that did all the talking.

It pleased Darius to appoint 120 satraps to rule throughout the kingdom, with three administrators over them, one of whom was Daniel. The satraps were made accountable to them so that the king might not suffer loss. Now Daniel so distinguished himself among the administrators and the satraps by his exceptional qualities that the king planned to set him over the whole kingdom. At this, the administrators and the satraps tried to find grounds for charges against Daniel in his conduct of government affairs, but they were unable to do so. They could find no corruption in him, because he was trustworthy and neither corrupt nor negligent. Finally these men said, "We will never find any basis for charges against this man Daniel unless it has something to do with the law of his God."

So these administrators and satraps went as a group to the king and said: "May King Darius live forever! The royal administrators, prefects, satraps, advisers and governors have all agreed that the king should issue an edict and enforce the decree that anyone who prays to any god or human being during the next thirty days, except to you, Your Majesty, shall be thrown into the lions' den. Now, Your Majesty, issue the decree and put it in writing so that it cannot be altered — in accordance with the law of the Medes and Persians, which cannot be repealed." So King Darius put the decree in writing.

Now when Daniel learned that the decree had been published, he went home to his upstairs room where the windows opened toward Jerusalem. Three times a day he got down on his knees and prayed, giving thanks to his God, just as he had done before. Then these men went as a group and found Daniel praying and asking God for help. So they went to the king and spoke to him about his royal decree: "Did you not publish a decree that during the next thirty days anyone who prays to any god or human being except to you, Your Majesty, would be thrown into the lions' den?"

The king answered, "The decree stands — in accordance with the law of the Medes and Persians, which cannot be repealed."

Then they said to the king, "Daniel, who is one of the exiles from Judah, pays no attention to you, Your Majesty, or to the decree you put in writing. He still prays three times a day." When the king heard this, he was greatly distressed; he was determined to rescue Daniel and made every effort until sundown to save him.

Then the men went as a group to King Darius

and said to him, "Remember, Your Majesty, that according to the law of the Medes and Persians no decree or edict that the king issues can be changed."

So the king gave the order, and they brought Daniel and threw him into the lions' den. The king said to Daniel, "May your God, whom you serve continually, rescue you!"

A stone was brought and placed over the mouth of the den, and the king sealed it with his own signet ring and with the rings of his nobles, so that Daniel's situation might not be changed. Then the king returned to his palace and spent the night without eating and without any entertainment being brought to him. And he could not sleep.

At the first light of dawn, the king got up and hurried to the lions' den. When he came near the den, he called to Daniel in an anguished voice, "Daniel, servant of the living God, has your God, whom you serve continually, been able to rescue you from the lions?"

Daniel answered, "May the king live forever! My God sent his angel, and he shut the mouths of the lions. They have not hurt me, because I was found innocent in his sight. Nor have I ever done any wrong before you, Your Majesty."

The king was overjoyed and gave orders to lift Daniel out of the den. And when Daniel was lifted from the den, no wound was found on him, because he had trusted in his God.

At the king's command, the men who had falsely accused Daniel were brought in and thrown into the lions' den, along with their wives and children. And before they reached the floor of the den, the lions overpowered them and crushed all their bones.

Then King Darius wrote to all the nations and peoples of every language in all the earth:

"May you prosper greatly!

"I issue a decree that in every part of my kingdom people must fear and reverence the God of Daniel.

"For he is the living God
    and he endures forever;
his kingdom will not be destroyed,
    his dominion will never end.
He rescues and he saves;
    he performs signs and wonders
    in the heavens and on the earth.
He has rescued Daniel
    from the power of the lions."

God's signs and wonders are undeniably awe-inspiring. In the book of Acts, Paul's and Silas's boldness got them thrown into jail; then as they lifted their voices in prayers and singing hymns of worship during the night, a sudden earthquake resulted in their release.

Once when we were going to the place of prayer, we were met by a female slave who had a spirit by which she predicted the future. She earned a great deal of money for her owners by fortune-telling. She followed Paul and the rest of us, shouting, "These men are servants of the Most High God, who are telling you the way to be saved." She kept this up for many days. Finally Paul became so annoyed that he turned around and said to the spirit, "In the name of Jesus Christ I command you to come out of her!" At that moment the spirit left her.

When her owners realized that their hope of making money was gone, they seized Paul and Silas and dragged them into the marketplace to face the authorities. They brought them before the magistrates and said, "These men are Jews, and are throwing our city into an uproar by advocating customs unlawful for us Romans to accept or practice."

The crowd joined in the attack against Paul and Silas, and the magistrates ordered them to be stripped and beaten with rods. After they had been severely flogged, they were thrown into prison, and the jailer was commanded to guard them carefully. When he received these orders, he put them in the inner cell and fastened their feet in the stocks.

About midnight Paul and Silas were praying and singing hymns to God, and the other prisoners were listening to them. Suddenly there was such a violent earthquake that the foundations of the prison were shaken. At once all the prison doors flew open, and everyone's chains came loose. The jailer woke up, and when he saw the prison doors open, he drew his sword and was about to kill himself because he thought the prisoners had escaped. But Paul shouted, "Don't harm yourself! We are all here!"

The jailer called for lights, rushed in and fell trembling before Paul and Silas. He then brought them out and asked, "Sirs, what must I do to be saved?"

They replied, "Believe in the Lord Jesus, and you will be saved — you and your household." Then they spoke the word of the Lord to him and to all the others in his house. At that hour of the night the jailer took them and washed their wounds; then immediately he and all his household were baptized. The jailer brought them into his house and set a meal before them; he was filled with joy because he had come to believe in God — he and his whole household.

When it was daylight, the magistrates sent

their officers to the jailer with the order: "Release those men."

WORSHIPING TOGETHER

A relationship with God can be both a private and a personal experience, but much of worship is meant to be practiced in community. God is a community within himself (Father, Son and Holy Spirit), and his Word encourages us to gather with other believers to encourage one another, pray together and remember God's love for us. After the crucifixion, death and resurrection of Jesus, the dynamics of communal worship changed drastically. Animal sacrifices are no longer required to restore a relationship with God. Instead, through Jesus' blood, shed as a voluntary sacrifice, those who repent and accept Jesus as their Savior will have their sins forgiven.

The law is only a shadow of the good things that are coming — not the realities themselves. For this reason it can never, by the same sacrifices repeated endlessly year after year, make perfect those who draw near to worship. Otherwise, would they not have stopped being offered? For the worshipers would have been cleansed once for all, and would no longer have felt guilty for their sins. But those sacrifices are an annual reminder of sins. It is impossible for the blood of bulls and goats to take away sins.

Therefore, when Christ came into the world, he said:

> "Sacrifice and offering you did not desire,
>   but a body you prepared for me;
> with burnt offerings and sin offerings
>   you were not pleased.
> Then I said, 'Here I am — it is written
>   about me in the scroll —
> I have come to do your will, my God.'"

First he said, "Sacrifices and offerings, burnt offerings and sin offerings you did not desire, nor were you pleased with them" — though they were offered in accordance with the law. Then he said, "Here I am, I have come to do your will." He sets aside the first to establish the second. And by that will, we have been made holy through the sacrifice of the body of Jesus Christ once for all.

Day after day every priest stands and performs his religious duties; again and again he offers the same sacrifices, which can never take away sins. But when this priest had offered for all time one sacrifice for sins, he sat down at the right hand of God, and since that time he waits for his enemies to be made his footstool. For by one sacrifice he has made perfect forever those who are being made holy.

The Holy Spirit also testifies to us about this. First he says:

> "This is the covenant I will make with
>   them
>   after that time, says the Lord.
> I will put my laws in their hearts,
>   and I will write them on their
>   minds."

Then he adds:

> "Their sins and lawless acts
>   I will remember no more."

And where these have been forgiven, sacrifice for sin is no longer necessary.

Therefore, brothers and sisters, since we have confidence to enter the Most Holy Place by the blood of Jesus, by a new and living way opened for us through the curtain, that is, his body, and since we have a great priest [Jesus] over the house of God, let us draw near to God with a sincere heart and with the full assurance that faith brings, having our hearts sprinkled to cleanse us from a guilty conscience and having our bodies washed with pure water. Let us hold unswervingly to the hope we profess, for he who promised is faithful. And let us consider how we may spur one another on toward love and good deeds, not giving up meeting together, as some are in the habit of doing, but encouraging one another — and all the more as you see the Day approaching.

The Lord's Supper essentially replaced the practice of animal sacrifice in the New Testament church. When believers gather to pray, sing and learn, they break bread and share a cup of wine as a way of remembering Christ's love for them. Jesus introduced this new practice to his disciples the night before his crucifixion.

Then came the day of Unleavened Bread on which the Passover lamb had to be sacrificed. Jesus sent Peter and John, saying, "Go and make preparations for us to eat the Passover."

"Where do you want us to prepare for it?" they asked.

He replied, "As you enter the city, a man carrying a jar of water will meet you. Follow him to the house that he enters, and say to the owner of the house, 'The Teacher asks: Where is the guest room, where I may eat the Passover with my disciples?' He will show you a large room upstairs, all furnished. Make preparations there."

They left and found things just as Jesus had told them. So they prepared the Passover.

When the hour came, Jesus and his apostles reclined at the table. And he said to them, "I have eagerly desired to eat this Passover with you before I suffer. For I tell you, I will not eat it again until it finds fulfillment in the kingdom of God."

After taking the cup, he gave thanks and said, "Take this and divide it among you. For I tell you I will not drink again from the fruit of the vine until the kingdom of God comes."

And he took bread, gave thanks and broke it, and gave it to them, saying, "This is my body given for you; do this in remembrance of me."

In the same way, after the supper he took the cup, saying, "This cup is the new covenant in my blood, which is poured out for you. But the hand of him who is going to betray me is with mine on the table. The Son of Man will go as it has been decreed. But woe to that man who betrays him!" They began to question among themselves which of them it might be who would do this.

A dispute also arose among them as to which of them was considered to be greatest. Jesus said to them, "The kings of the Gentiles lord it over them; and those who exercise authority over them call themselves Benefactors. But you are not to be like that. Instead, the greatest among you should be like the youngest, and the one who rules like the one who serves. For who is greater, the one who is at the table or the one who serves? Is it not the one who is at the table? But I am among you as one who serves. You are those who have stood by me in my trials. And I confer on you a kingdom, just as my Father conferred one on me, so that you may eat and drink at my table in my kingdom and sit on thrones, judging the twelve tribes of Israel."

Of course, believers can also honor Jesus' sacrifice every day in the way that they choose to live. While under house arrest in Rome, the apostle Paul wrote to the Christians in the city of Colossae. He encouraged them to throw off their old self-centered way of living and commit to live their new lives solely for the purpose of worshiping and serving God. Paul's instructions were not addressed to individual worshipers, but to the worship community as a whole.

Since, then, you have been raised with Christ, set your hearts on things above, where Christ is, seated at the right hand of God. Set your minds on things above, not on earthly things. For you died, and your life is now hidden with Christ in God. When Christ, who is your life, appears, then you also will appear with him in glory.

Put to death, therefore, whatever belongs to your earthly nature: sexual immorality, impurity, lust, evil desires and greed, which is idolatry. Because of these, the wrath of God is coming. You used to walk in these ways, in the life you once lived. But now you must also rid yourselves of all such things as these: anger, rage, malice, slander, and filthy language from your lips. Do not lie to each other, since you have taken off your old self with its practices and have put on the new self, which is being renewed in knowledge in the image of its Creator. Here there is no Gentile or Jew, circumcised or uncircumcised, barbarian, Scythian, slave or free, but Christ is all, and is in all.

Therefore, as God's chosen people, holy and dearly loved, clothe yourselves with compassion, kindness, humility, gentleness and patience. Bear with each other and forgive one another if any of you has a grievance against someone. Forgive as the Lord forgave you. And over all these virtues put on love, which binds them all together in perfect unity.

Let the peace of Christ rule in your hearts, since as members of one body you were called to peace. And be thankful. Let the message of Christ dwell among you richly as you teach and admonish one another with all wisdom through psalms, hymns, and songs from the Spirit, singing to God with gratitude in your hearts. And whatever you do, whether in word or deed, do it all in the name of the Lord Jesus, giving thanks to God the Father through him.

CHAPTER

3

Joy

KEY IDEA

Despite my circumstances,
I feel inner contentment and understand
my purpose in life.

KEY VERSE

I have told you this so that my joy may be in you
and that your joy may be complete.
John 15:11

SOURCE OF JOY

*God may shower us with blessings and circum-
stances that bring joy to our lives, but true joy is
found not in those things themselves but in their
source. Joy can also be fueled and found in living out God's Word and trusting in the promises
God gives us in his Word. The psalmist declared
this truth with great confidence in this song.*

Keep me safe, my God,
    for in you I take refuge.

I say to the LORD, "You are my Lord;
    apart from you I have no good thing."
I say of the holy people who are in the
        land,
    "They are the noble ones in whom is
        all my delight."
Those who run after other gods will
        suffer more and more.
    I will not pour out libations of blood to
        such gods
    or take up their names on my lips.

LORD, you alone are my portion and
        my cup;
    you make my lot secure.
The boundary lines have fallen for me in
        pleasant places;
    surely I have a delightful inheritance.

I will praise the LORD, who counsels me;
   even at night my heart instructs me.
I keep my eyes always on the LORD.
    With him at my right hand, I will not
      be shaken.

Therefore my heart is glad and my tongue
      rejoices;
   my body also will rest secure,
because you will not abandon me to the
      realm of the dead,
   nor will you let your faithful one see
      decay.
You make known to me the path of life;
   you will fill me with joy in your
      presence,
   with eternal pleasures at your right
      hand.

The precepts of the LORD are right,
   giving joy to the heart.
The commands of the LORD are radiant,
   giving light to the eyes.

I rejoice in following your statutes
   as one rejoices in great riches.

I rejoice in your promise
   like one who finds great spoil.

God's promises find their ultimate fulfillment in his Son Jesus. So when we abide in the vine of Christ through obedience to his commands, his nutrients of joy run through our spiritual veins from the inside out and produce the ripe, juicy fruit of joy in and through our lives.

"I am the true vine, and my Father is the gardener. He cuts off every branch in me that bears no fruit, while every branch that does bear fruit he prunes so that it will be even more fruitful. You are already clean because of the word I have spoken to you. Remain in me, as I also remain in you. No branch can bear fruit by itself; it must remain in the vine. Neither can you bear fruit unless you remain in me.

"I am the vine; you are the branches. If you remain in me and I in you, you will bear much fruit; apart from me you can do nothing. If you do not remain in me, you are like a branch that is thrown away and withers; such branches are picked up, thrown into the fire and burned. If you remain in me and my words remain in you, ask whatever you wish, and it will be done for you. This is to my Father's glory, that you bear much fruit, showing yourselves to be my disciples.

"As the Father has loved me, so have I loved you. Now remain in my love. If you keep my commands, you will remain in my love, just as I have kept my Father's commands and remain in his love. I have told you this so that my joy may be in you and that your joy may be complete."

James wrote one of the first letters in the New Testament that instructed believers regarding this new life in Christ. Followers of Jesus can not only experience joy in spite of trials, but the trials themselves can be beneficial because they force us back to the true source of joy — God.

Consider it pure joy, my brothers and sisters, whenever you face trials of many kinds, because you know that the testing of your faith produces perseverance. Let perseverance finish its work so that you may be mature and complete, not lacking anything. If any of you lacks wisdom, you should ask God, who gives generously to all without finding fault, and it will be given to you. But when you ask, you must believe and not doubt, because the one who doubts is like a wave of the sea, blown and tossed by the wind. That person should not expect to receive anything from the Lord. Such a person is double-minded and unstable in all they do.

Believers in humble circumstances ought to take pride in their high position. But the rich should take pride in their humiliation — since they will pass away like a wild flower. For the sun rises with scorching heat and withers the plant; its blossom falls and its beauty is destroyed. In the same way, the rich will fade away even while they go about their business.

Blessed is the one who perseveres under trial because, having stood the test, that person will receive the crown of life that the Lord has promised to those who love him.

When tempted, no one should say, "God is tempting me." For God cannot be tempted by evil, nor does he tempt anyone; but each person is tempted when they are dragged away by their own evil desire and enticed. Then, after desire has conceived, it gives birth to sin; and sin, when it is full-grown, gives birth to death.

Don't be deceived, my dear brothers and sisters. Every good and perfect gift is from above, coming down from the Father of the heavenly lights, who does not change like shifting shadows.

JOYFUL CELEBRATIONS

In the Old Testament people often responded to God's blessings with joyful celebrations. Coming together intentionally to remember God stimulated joy in the hearts of the people. The annual Festival of Tabernacles especially provided an opportunity for the Israelites to celebrate God's goodness, since the focus was the blessing of God on their harvest and the work

*of their hands. Moses instructed the Israelites to
make this festival an occasion to express their
joy.*

Celebrate the Festival of Tabernacles for seven
days after you have gathered the produce of your
threshing floor and your winepress. Be joyful at
your festival — you, your sons and daughters, your
male and female servants, and the Levites, the for-
eigners, the fatherless and the widows who live in
your towns. For seven days celebrate the festival
to the LORD your God at the place the LORD will
choose. For the LORD your God will bless you in
all your harvest and in all the work of your hands,
and your joy will be complete.

Three times a year all your men must appear
before the LORD your God at the place he will
choose: at the Festival of Unleavened Bread, the
Festival of Weeks and the Festival of Tabernacles.
No one should appear before the LORD empty-
handed: Each of you must bring a gift in propor-
tion to the way the LORD your God has blessed you.

*Another joyful celebration recorded in the Old
Testament occurred when David retrieved the
ark of the covenant from the Philistines. David
understood the power of God's presence in
the center of Israelite life and community. After
he built a tent to store the ark he wrote a grand*

song to celebrate God for who he is and what he had consistently done for Israel.

David first appointed Asaph and his associates to give praise to the LORD in this manner:

> Give praise to the LORD, proclaim his
>   name;
>   make known among the nations what
>   he has done.
> Sing to him, sing praise to him;
>   tell of all his wonderful acts.
> Glory in his holy name;
>   let the hearts of those who seek the
>   LORD rejoice.
> Look to the LORD and his strength;
>   seek his face always.
>
> Remember the wonders he has done,
>   his miracles, and the judgments he
>   pronounced,
> you his servants, the descendants of
>   Israel,
>   his chosen ones, the children of Jacob.
> He is the LORD our God;
>   his judgments are in all the earth.
>
> He remembers his covenant forever,
>   the promise he made, for a thousand
>   generations,

the covenant he made with Abraham,
    the oath he swore to Isaac.
He confirmed it to Jacob as a decree,
    to Israel as an everlasting covenant:
"To you I will give the land of Canaan
    as the portion you will inherit."

When they were but few in number,
    few indeed, and strangers in it,
they wandered from nation to nation,
    from one kingdom to another.
He allowed no one to oppress them;
    for their sake he rebuked kings:
"Do not touch my anointed ones;
    do my prophets no harm."

Sing to the LORD, all the earth;
    proclaim his salvation day after day.
Declare his glory among the nations,
    his marvelous deeds among all
        peoples.

For great is the LORD and most worthy
        of praise;
    he is to be feared above all gods.
For all the gods of the nations are idols,
    but the LORD made the heavens.
Splendor and majesty are before him;
    strength and joy are in his dwelling
        place.

Ascribe to the LORD, all you families of
      nations,
  ascribe to the LORD glory and
      strength.
Ascribe to the LORD the glory due his
      name;
  bring an offering and come before
      him.
Worship the LORD in the splendor of
      his holiness.
  Tremble before him, all the earth!
  The world is firmly established; it
      cannot be moved.

Let the heavens rejoice, let the earth be
      glad;
  let them say among the nations, "The
      LORD reigns!"
Let the sea resound, and all that is in it;
  let the fields be jubilant, and everything
      in them!
Let the trees of the forest sing,
  let them sing for joy before the LORD,
  for he comes to judge the earth.

Give thanks to the LORD, for he is good;
  his love endures forever.
Cry out, "Save us, God our Savior;
  gather us and deliver us from the
      nations,

that we may give thanks to your holy
name,
and glory in your praise."
Praise be to the LORD, the God of Israel,
from everlasting to everlasting.

Then all the people said "Amen" and "Praise the
LORD."

*A little over 350 years after the death of David,
the Babylonians exiled the people of Israel from
the southern kingdom of Judah. The magnifi-
cent temple built by David's son Solomon was
destroyed. Roughly 70 years later, according to
God's plan, the people began to return home
and immediately started rebuilding the temple.
Opposition from the neighboring people, however, brought the project to a halt. God wielded
the heart of a foreign ruler with immense power,
King Darius of Persia (also known as the king of
Assyria), to demand the opposition stand down
and allow the temple to be completed. Finally,
20 years after the work began, the second temple was completed. With joy the returned exiles
dedicated the temple and then about a month
later celebrated the Passover (a yearly festival
commemorating the night in Egypt when God
"passed over" all the Israelites who had the
blood of a lamb on the doorpost of their homes,
thus sparing the lives of their firstborn sons) and*

the Festival of Unleavened Bread (a seven-day festival beginning the day after Passover where the Israelites ate only unleavened bread and presented their first fruits of the harvest to the priests).

Because of the decree King Darius had sent, Tattenai, governor of Trans-Euphrates, and She-thar-Bozenai and their associates carried it out with diligence. So the elders of the Jews continued to build and prosper under the preaching of Haggai the prophet and Zechariah, a descendant of Iddo. They finished building the temple according to the command of the God of Israel and the decrees of Cyrus, Darius and Artaxerxes, kings of Persia. The temple was completed on the third day of the month Adar, in the sixth year of the reign of King Darius.

Then the people of Israel — the priests, the Levites and the rest of the exiles — celebrated the dedication of the house of God with joy. For the dedication of this house of God they offered a hundred bulls, two hundred rams, four hundred male lambs and, as a sin offering for all Israel, twelve male goats, one for each of the tribes of Israel. And they installed the priests in their divisions and the Levites in their groups for the service of God at Jerusalem, according to what is written in the Book of Moses.

On the fourteenth day of the first month, the exiles celebrated the Passover. The priests and Levites had purified themselves and were all ceremonially clean. The Levites slaughtered the Passover lamb for all the exiles, for their relatives the priests and for themselves. So the Israelites who had returned from the exile ate it, together with all who had separated themselves from the unclean practices of their Gentile neighbors in order to seek the LORD, the God of Israel. For seven days they celebrated with joy the Festival of Unleavened Bread, because the LORD had filled them with joy by changing the attitude of the king of Assyria so that he assisted them in the work on the house of God, the God of Israel.

JOY DESPITE OUR CIRCUMSTANCES

Prior to the exile and return of the southern kingdom of Judah was a dark season. The people were led, almost without interruption, by a succession of evil kings. Habakkuk was a prophet trying desperately to get the people back on track. He asked God how long he was going to let injustice and wickedness go on before he disciplined the nation. God informed the prophet that he was going to use the Babylonians to deal with Judah's persistent disobedience. Habakkuk struggled with this idea at first but in the end found resolve.

*Even though God's people were going to go
through a difficult season, Habakkuk knew they
could retain their joy based on what God had
done for them in the past and his promises for
the future.*

LORD, I have heard of your fame;
    I stand in awe of your deeds, LORD.
Repeat them in our day,
    in our time make them known;
    in wrath remember mercy.

God came from Teman,
    the Holy One from Mount Paran.
His glory covered the heavens
    and his praise filled the earth.
His splendor was like the sunrise;
    rays flashed from his hand,
    where his power was hidden.
Plague went before him;
    pestilence followed his steps.
He stood, and shook the earth;
    he looked, and made the nations
        tremble.
The ancient mountains crumbled
    and the age-old hills collapsed —
    but he marches on forever.
I saw the tents of Cushan in distress,
    the dwellings of Midian in anguish.

Were you angry with the rivers, LORD?
   Was your wrath against the streams?
Did you rage against the sea
   when you rode your horses
   and your chariots to victory?
You uncovered your bow,
   you called for many arrows.
You split the earth with rivers;
   the mountains saw you and writhed.
Torrents of water swept by;
   the deep roared
   and lifted its waves on high.

Sun and moon stood still in the heavens
   at the glint of your flying arrows,
   at the lightning of your flashing
      spear.
In wrath you strode through the earth
   and in anger you threshed the nations.
You came out to deliver your people,
   to save your anointed one.
You crushed the leader of the land of
      wickedness,
   you stripped him from head to foot.
With his own spear you pierced his head
   when his warriors stormed out to
      scatter us,
gloating as though about to devour
   the wretched who were in hiding.

You trampled the sea with your horses,
   churning the great waters.

I heard and my heart pounded,
   my lips quivered at the sound;
decay crept into my bones,
   and my legs trembled.
Yet I will wait patiently for the day of
      calamity
   to come on the nation invading us.
Though the fig tree does not bud
   and there are no grapes on the vines,
though the olive crop fails
   and the fields produce no food,
though there are no sheep in the pen
   and no cattle in the stalls,
yet I will rejoice in the LORD,
   I will be joyful in God my Savior.

The Sovereign LORD is my strength;
   he makes my feet like the feet of a deer,
   he enables me to tread on the heights.

Just as God's people found joy and strength in God's promises amid dark times during Habakkuk's day, Jesus' disciples drew comfort and strength from Jesus' promises as they prepared for his death. A few hours before he was crucified Jesus sat with them and reassured them that their grief would be short-lived—three days to be exact. After that time something was going to happen to secure their joy in any and all circumstances.

It was just before the Passover Festival. Jesus knew that the hour had come for him to leave this world and go to the Father. Having loved his own who were in the world, he loved them to the end.

Jesus went on to say, "In a little while you will see me no more, and then after a little while you will see me."

At this, some of his disciples said to one another, "What does he mean by saying, 'In a little while you will see me no more, and then after a little while you will see me,' and 'Because I am going to the Father'?" They kept asking, "What does he mean by 'a little while'? We don't understand what he is saying."

Jesus saw that they wanted to ask him about this, so he said to them, "Are you asking one another what I meant when I said, 'In a little while you will see me no more, and then after a little while you will see me'? Very truly I tell you, you will weep and mourn while the world rejoices. You will grieve, but your grief will turn to joy. A woman giving birth to a child has pain because her time has come; but when her baby is born she forgets the anguish because of her joy that a child is born into the world. So with you: Now is your time of grief, but I will see you again and you will rejoice, and no one will take away your joy. In that day you will no longer ask me anything. Very truly I tell you, my Father will give you whatever you ask in my name. Until now you have not asked for anything in my name. Ask and you will receive, and your joy will be complete."

One of those disciples, the apostle Paul, later wrote a joyful treatise of sorts while under house arrest and chained to a Roman guard. In a passionate letter to the church at Philippi, Paul fervently expressed his joy in Christ. Half of the lessons on increasing our joy are "taught" explicitly by Paul. Half of the lessons are "caught" implicitly by observing how Paul found joy despite his circumstances. At the letter's opening, notice how he found joy in the people God had placed in his life. Then we learn that Paul even saw his imprisonment as a blessing, for it helped bring attention to the gospel message.

Paul and Timothy, servants of Christ Jesus,

To all God's holy people in Christ Jesus at Philippi, together with the overseers and deacons:

Grace and peace to you from God our Father and the Lord Jesus Christ.

I thank my God every time I remember you. In all my prayers for all of you, I always pray with joy because of your partnership in the gospel from the first day until now, being confident of this, that he who began a good work in you will carry it on to completion until the day of Christ Jesus.

It is right for me to feel this way about all of you, since I have you in my heart and, whether I am in chains or defending and confirming the gospel, all of you share in God's grace with me. God can testify how I long for all of you with the affection of Christ Jesus.

And this is my prayer: that your love may abound more and more in knowledge and depth of insight, so that you may be able to discern what is best and may be pure and blameless for the day of Christ, filled with the fruit of righteousness that comes through Jesus Christ — to the glory and praise of God.

Now I want you to know, brothers and sisters, that what has happened to me has actually served to advance the gospel. As a result, it has become clear throughout the whole palace guard and to everyone else that I am in chains for Christ. And because of my chains, most of the brothers and sisters have become confident in the Lord and dare all the more to proclaim the gospel without fear.

It is true that some preach Christ out of envy and rivalry, but others out of goodwill. The latter do so out of love, knowing that I am put here for the defense of the gospel. The former preach Christ out of selfish ambition, not sincerely, supposing that they can stir up trouble for me while I am in chains. But what does it matter? The important thing is that in every way, whether from false motives or true, Christ is preached. And because of this I rejoice.

Yes, and I will continue to rejoice, for I know that through your prayers and God's provision of the Spirit of Jesus Christ what has happened to me will turn out for my deliverance.

Paul also instructed the Philippian believers on how to rise above the fear spurred by those who opposed them. He invited them to remove grumbling and arguing from their vocabulary as a means to increase their joy. The ultimate source of joy is in knowing Christ better, so Paul encouraged his readers to put the past behind them and stay focused on the future, giving all their troubles to God and rehearsing his blessings continuously.

Whatever happens, conduct yourselves in a manner worthy of the gospel of Christ. Then, whether I come and see you or only hear about you in my absence, I will know that you stand firm in the one Spirit, striving together as one for the faith of the gospel without being frightened in any way by those who oppose you. This is a sign to them that they will be destroyed, but that you will be saved — and that by God. For it has been granted to you on behalf of Christ not only to believe in him, but also to suffer for him, since you are going through the same struggle you saw I had, and now hear that I still have.

Therefore, my dear friends, as you have always obeyed — not only in my presence, but now much more in my absence — continue to work out your salvation with fear and trembling, for it is God who works in you to will and to act in order to fulfill his good purpose.

Do everything without grumbling or arguing, so that you may become blameless and pure, "children of God without fault in a warped and crooked generation." Then you will shine among them like stars in the sky as you hold firmly to the word of life. And then I will be able to boast on the day of Christ that I did not run or labor in vain. But even if I am being poured out like a drink offering on the sacrifice and service coming from your faith, I am glad and rejoice with all of you. So you too should be glad and rejoice with me.

Further, my brothers and sisters, rejoice in the Lord! It is no trouble for me to write the same things to you again, and it is a safeguard for you.

Watch out for those dogs, those evildoers, those mutilators of the flesh. For it is we who are the circumcision, we who serve God by his Spirit, who boast in Christ Jesus, and who put no confidence in the flesh — though I myself have reasons for such confidence.

If someone else thinks they have reasons to put confidence in the flesh, I have more: circumcised on the eighth day, of the people of Israel, of the tribe of Benjamin, a Hebrew of Hebrews; in regard to the law, a Pharisee; as for zeal, persecuting the church; as for righteousness based on the law, faultless.

But whatever were gains to me I now consider loss for the sake of Christ. What is more, I consider everything a loss because of the surpassing worth of knowing Christ Jesus my Lord, for whose sake I have lost all things. I consider them garbage, that I may gain Christ and be found in him, not having a righteousness of my own that comes from the law, but that which is through faith in Christ — the righteousness that comes from God on the basis of faith. I want to know Christ — yes, to know the power of his resurrection and participation in his sufferings, becoming like him in his death, and so, somehow, attaining to the resurrection from the dead.

Not that I have already obtained all this, or have already arrived at my goal, but I press on to take hold of that for which Christ Jesus took hold of me. Brothers and sisters, I do not consider myself yet to have taken hold of it. But one thing I do: Forgetting what is behind and straining toward what is ahead, I press on toward the goal to win the prize for which God has called me heavenward in Christ Jesus.

All of us, then, who are mature should take such a view of things. And if on some point you think differently, that too God will make clear to you. Only let us live up to what we have already attained.

Join together in following my example, brothers and sisters, and just as you have us as a model, keep your eyes on those who live as we do. For, as I have often told you before and now tell you again even with tears, many live as enemies of the cross of Christ. Their destiny is destruction, their god is their stomach, and their glory is in their shame. Their mind is set on earthly things. But our citizenship is in heaven. And we eagerly await a Savior from there, the Lord Jesus Christ, who, by the power that enables him to bring everything under his control, will transform our lowly bodies so that they will be like his glorious body.

Therefore, my brothers and sisters, you whom I love and long for, my joy and crown, stand firm in the Lord in this way, dear friends!

I plead with Euodia and I plead with Syntyche to be of the same mind in the Lord. Yes, and I ask you, my true companion, help these women since they have contended at my side in the cause of the gospel, along with Clement and the rest of my co-workers, whose names are in the book of life.

Rejoice in the Lord always. I will say it again: Rejoice! Let your gentleness be evident to all. The Lord is near. Do not be anxious about anything, but in every situation, by prayer and petition, with thanksgiving, present your requests to God. And the peace of God, which transcends all under-standing, will guard your hearts and your minds in Christ Jesus.

Finally, brothers and sisters, whatever is true, whatever is noble, whatever is right, whatever is pure, whatever is lovely, whatever is admirable — if anything is excellent or praiseworthy — think about such things. Whatever you have learned or received or heard from me, or seen in me — put it into practice. And the God of peace will be with you.

Paul wrapped up his thoughts by disclosing the secret to contentment despite life's varying cir-cumstances.

I rejoiced greatly in the Lord that at last you renewed your concern for me. Indeed, you were concerned, but you had no opportunity to show it. I am not saying this because I am in need, for I have learned to be content whatever the circumstances. I know what it is to be in need, and I know what it is to have plenty. I have learned the secret of being content in any and every situation, whether well fed or hungry, whether living in plenty or in want. I can do all this through him who gives me strength.

Like Paul, the apostle Peter also taught through his letters to the Christians scattered throughout Asia Minor that believers are in a position to experience joy in spite of, and because of, their difficult circumstances. The same is true for followers of Jesus today.

Praise be to the God and Father of our Lord Jesus Christ! In his great mercy he has given us new birth into a living hope through the resurrection of Jesus Christ from the dead, and into an inheritance that can never perish, spoil or fade. This inheritance is kept in heaven for you, who through faith are shielded by God's power until the coming of the salvation that is ready to be revealed in the last time. In all this you greatly rejoice, though now for a little while you may have had to suffer grief in all kinds of trials. These have come so that the proven genuineness of your faith — of greater worth than gold, which perishes even though refined by fire — may result in praise, glory and honor when Jesus Christ is revealed. Though you have not seen him, you love him; and even though you do not see him now, you believe in him and are filled with an inexpressible and glorious joy, for you are receiving the end result of your faith, the salvation of your souls.

Dear friends, do not be surprised at the fiery ordeal that has come on you to test you, as though something strange were happening to you. But rejoice inasmuch as you participate in the sufferings of Christ, so that you may be overjoyed when his glory is revealed. If you are insulted because of the name of Christ, you are blessed, for the Spirit of glory and of God rests on you. If you suffer, it should not be as a murderer or thief or any other kind of criminal, or even as a meddler. However, if you suffer as a Christian, do not be ashamed, but praise God that you bear that name.

Humble yourselves, therefore, under God's mighty hand, that he may lift you up in due time. Cast all your anxiety on him because he cares for you.

Be alert and of sober mind. Your enemy the devil prowls around like a roaring lion looking for someone to devour. Resist him, standing firm in the faith, because you know that the family of believers throughout the world is undergoing the same kind of sufferings.

And the God of all grace, who called you to his eternal glory in Christ, after you have suffered a little while, will himself restore you and make you strong, firm and steadfast. To him be the power for ever and ever. Amen.

Chart of References

CHAPTER 1: PERSONAL GOD

Genesis 16:1–16
Genesis 21:1–21
Psalm 8:1–9
Psalm 23:1–6
Psalm 139:1–24
Psalm 145:1–21

2 Kings 20:1–7
Jeremiah 1:1–19
Jeremiah 29:1–14
Matthew 6:25–34
Romans 8:12–39
James 1:1–18

CHAPTER 2: WORSHIP

Psalm 95:1–7
Isaiah 1:11–20
Matthew 23:1–28
Exodus 15:1–21
Daniel 6:1–27

Acts 16:16–35
Hebrews 10:1–25
Luke 22:7–30
Colossians 3:1–17

CHAPTER 3: JOY

Psalm 16:1–11
Psalm 19:8
Psalm 119:14
Psalm 119:162
John 15:1–11
James 1:2–17
Deuteronomy 16:13–17
1 Chronicles 16:7–36
Ezra 6:13–22
Habakkuk 3:1–19
John 13:1

John 16:16–24
Philippians 1:1–19
Philippians 1:27–30
Philippians 2:12–18
Philippians 3:1–21
Philippians 4:1–9
Philippians 4:10–13
1 Peter 1:3–9
1 Peter 4:12–16
1 Peter 5:6–11

BELIEVE

POWERED BY **ZONDERVAN**

Dear Reader,

Notable researcher George Gallup Jr. summarized his findings on the state of American Christianity with this startling revelation: **"The stark fact is, many Christians don't know what they believe or why."**

The problem is not that people lack a hunger for God's Word. Research tells us that the number one thing people want from their church is for it to help them understand the Bible, and that Bible engagement is the number one catalyst for spiritual growth. Nothing else comes close.

This is why I am passionate about *Believe*—a Bible engagement experience to anchor every member of your family in the key teachings of the Bible.

Grounded in Scripture, *Believe* is a spiritual growth experience that helps people of all ages become more like Jesus in their beliefs, actions, and character.

When these timeless truths are understood, believed in the heart, and applied to our daily living, they can transform a life, a family, a church, a city, a nation, and even our world.

Imagine thousands of churches and countless individuals all over the world finally able to declare—**"I know what I believe and why, and in God's strength I will seek to live it out all the days of my life."**

It could change the world.

In Him,

Randy Frazee
General Editor, *Believe*

LIVING THE STORY OF THE BIBLE TO BECOME LIKE JESUS

Teach your whole family how to think, act, and be like Jesus!

- **Adults** – Unlocks the 10 key beliefs, 10 key practices, and 10 key virtues of a Christian. Curriculum also available.
- ***Think, Act, Be Like Jesus*** – This companion to *Believe* helps readers develop a personal vision and a simple plan for getting started on their spiritual growth journey.
- **Students** – Contains the same Scriptures as the adult edition, but with transitions and fun features to engage students. Curriculum also available.
- **Children** – With a Kids' Edition for ages 8-12, a Storybook for ages 4-8, and three levels of curriculum, children of all ages will learn how to think, act, and be like Jesus.
- **Churches** – *Believe* is flexible, affordable, and easy to use with your church, in any ministry, from nursery to adults...and even the whole church.
- **Spanish** – All *Believe* resources are also available in Spanish.

FOR ADULTS

9780310433583   9780310250173

FOR STUDENTS

9780310745617

FOR CHILDREN

9780310746010

9780310745907

FOR CHURCHES

Campaign Kit 9780310681717

WHAT YOU BELIEVE DRIVES EVERYTHING.

Grounded in Scripture, *Believe* is a topical abridgment of the NIV Bible, unlocking the 10 key beliefs, 10 key practices, and 10 key virtues that will help you become more like Jesus in your beliefs, actions, and character.

Learn the core truths of the Christian faith and how to live them out all the days of your life.

Know What You Believe and Why It Matters.

Hardcover   9780310433583

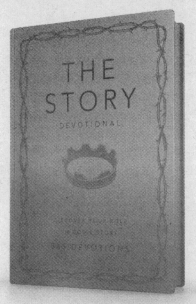

THE STORY DEVOTIONAL
Discover Your Role in God's Story

See your life and purpose in a whole new light—as part of God's epic story—with this beautiful leather-look devotional. Through 365 daily Scripture readings arranged chronologically, plus bite-sized reflections and a daily takeaway, this unique devotional illuminates how God has been weaving his plan throughout history. Each day, you'll be blessed with a reminder of God's unrelenting love and pursuit of his people.

Tan Leathersoft   9780310341895